# GREAT OLYMPIC MOMENTS

REVISED AND UPDATED

## Haydn Middleton

Heinemann
LIBRARY

## www.heinemann.co.uk/library

Visit our website to find out more information about Heinemann Library books.

To order:
☎ Phone 44 (0) 1865 888066
🗎 Send a fax to 44 (0)1865 314091
💻 Visit the Heinemann Library Bookshop at www.heinemann.co.uk/library to browse our catalogue and order online.

First published in Great Britain by Heinemann Library, Halley Court, Jordan Hill, Oxford OX2 8EJ, part of Harcourt Education. Heinemann Library is a registered trademark of Harcourt Education Ltd.

Editorial: Joanna Talbot
Design: Philippa Jenkins
Picture Research: Tracy Cummins
Production: Alison Parsons

Originated by Modern Age
Printed and bound in China by Leo Paper Group

ISBN 978 0 431 19159 1
12 11 10 09 08
10 9 8 7 6 5 4 3 2 1

**British Library Cataloguing in Publication Data**
Middleton, Haydn
    Great olympic moments. – (The olympics)
    1.Olympic games – Juvenile literature
    2.Olympics Records – Juvenile literature
    1.Title
    796.4·8

A full catalogue record for this book is available from the British Library.

**Acknowledgements**
The publishers would like to thank the following for permission to reproduce photographs:
Allsport: pp. **6**, **8**, **9**, **10**, **12**, **13**, **14**, **18**, **20**, **21**, **22**, **24**, **25**, **26**; AP Photo: pp. **7** (Vincent Thian), **11** (Kevork Djansezian), **15** (Thomas Kienzle), **28** (Anja Niedringhaus), **29** (Thanassis Stavrakis); Colorsport: pp. **16**, **19**; Corbis/Bettmann: p. **23**; Empics: p. **17**; Hulton Getty: p. **27**.

Cover photograph reproduced with permission of Adam Davy/EMPICS Sport/PA Photos.

The publishers would like to thank John Townsend for his assistance with the preparation of this book.

Every effort has been made to contact copyright holders of any material reproduced in this book. Any omissions will be rectified in subsequent printings if notice is given to the publishers.

# CONTENTS

Any words appearing in the text in bold, **like this**, are explained in the Glossary.

# INTRODUCTION

The modern Olympics began in 1896. Every Games since then has been lit up by marvellous sporting moments. The Olympic motto is '*Citius, Altius, Fortius*' – which is Latin for 'Swifter, Higher, Stronger'. In this book you can read about men and women – runners, jumpers, swimmers, gymnasts, skiers, footballers – who made that motto a reality in their own events. Sometimes they achieved success with style and ease. Sometimes they fought against terrific odds to come out on top. All of them won lasting, world-wide fame.

## THE JOY OF TAKING PART

For competitors and spectators alike, nothing quite compares with the thrill of an Olympic final. Britain's Sebastian Coe knows that as well as anyone. In 1980 and again in 1984 he won the 1,500 metres gold medal. 'There may be championships galore,' he wrote later, '... but to every young athlete who tied on his or her first pair of spikes in a draughty clubhouse in Sheffield, or a high-school trackside in Baltimore, or a corrugated-roofed changing room in a Nairobi suburb, it is the Olympic final that matters.'

But the Olympic Games has a second, longer and unofficial, motto. It was adapted from an American bishop's sermon in 1908, and it describes what could be called the true 'Olympic spirit': 'The most important thing in the Olympic Games is not to win but to take part, just as the most important thing in life is not the triumph but the struggle. The essential thing is not to have conquered but to have fought well.'

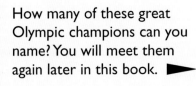

How many of these great Olympic champions can you name? You will meet them again later in this book. ▶

This might seem hard to believe nowadays. In our world, winning often seems to mean everything and coming second is often portrayed in the **media** as failure. But it need not be that way, as this little Olympic story shows.

## FROM ME TO YOU

Czech distance-runner Emil Zatopek was one of the greatest Olympians of all. In the early 1950s no one could match him, and at the Helsinki Games of 1952 he won three gold medals. Then in the 1960s another magnificent distance-runner emerged: Ron Clarke of Australia. Everyone knew Clarke was the world's best and he had the records to prove it. But although he gave his all at Tokyo in 1964 and at Mexico City in 1968 – and helped to make both Games so memorable – he came away without a single Olympic victory.

On his way back to Australia in 1966, he stopped over in Europe to see his old friend Emil Zatopek. On parting from him, Zatopek gave him a small gift, which Clarke opened only when he got home. Inside the wrapping was Zatopek's 10,000 metres gold medal from 1952. As Sebastian Coe points out: 'Zatopek, the kindest of men, well knew the important difference between failure and not winning. In that sense Ron Clarke had not failed, and the Olympic Games were richer for him.' In the pages that follow, you will meet many others who have truly enriched the Olympics.

## VENUES OF THE MODERN OLYMPIC GAMES

| Year | Summer Games | Winter Games |
| --- | --- | --- |
| 1896 | Athens, Greece | |
| 1900 | Paris, France | |
| 1904 | St Louis, USA | |
| 1908 | London, UK | |
| 1912 | Stockholm, Sweden | |
| 1916 | Games not held | |
| 1920 | Antwerp, Belgium | |
| 1924 | Paris, France | Chamonix, France |
| 1928 | Amsterdam, Netherlands | St Moritz, Switzerland |
| 1932 | Los Angeles, USA | Lake Placid, USA |
| 1936 | Berlin, Germany | Garmisch-Partenkirchen, Germany |
| 1940 | Games not held | Games not held |
| 1944 | Games not held | Games not held |
| 1948 | London, UK | St Moritz, Switzerland |
| 1952 | Helsinki, Finland | Oslo, Norway |
| 1956 | Melbourne, Australia | Cortina, Italy |
| 1960 | Rome, Italy | Squaw Valley, USA |
| 1964 | Tokyo, Japan | Innsbruck, Austria |
| 1968 | Mexico City, Mexico | Grenoble, France |
| 1972 | Munich, West Germany | Sapporo, Japan |
| 1976 | Montreal, Canada | Innsbruck, Austria |
| 1980 | Moscow, USSR | Lake Placid, USA |
| 1984 | Los Angeles, USA | Sarajevo, Yugoslavia (now Bosnia) |
| 1988 | Seoul, South Korea | Calgary, Canada |
| 1992 | Barcelona, Spain | Albertville, France |
| 1994 | | Lillehammer, Norway |
| 1996 | Atlanta, USA | |
| 1998 | | Nagano, Japan |
| 2000 | Sydney, Australia | |
| 2002 | | Salt Lake City, USA |
| 2004 | Athens, Greece | |
| 2006 | | Turin, Italy |
| 2008 | Beijing, China | |
| 2010 | | Vancouver, Canada |
| 2012 | London, UK | |

The Winter Games were not held until 1924. After 1992, the Summer and Winter Games have been held on a staggered two-year schedule.

# THE FASTEST MEN IN THE WORLD

For many sports fans, nothing can beat the sheer excitement of the two great Olympic sprint races – over 100 metres and 200 metres. The first Olympic 100 metres champion was an American, Thomas Burke, who won the 1896 race in Athens in 12.0 seconds. (To show how times change – 100 years later, at Atlanta, Canadian Donovan Bailey won the gold medal in a time of 9.84 seconds!)

Until 1924, Americans won every 100 metres title except one. All these winners were white men but more and more black athletes were going to American high schools and colleges, to get the necessary coaching to become great Olympians. At Los Angeles in 1932 Thomas 'Eddie' Tolan, a black sprinter from the University of Michigan, won gold in both the 100 metres and 200 metres. Four years later, his successor as Olympic sprint champion was perhaps *the* all-time great...

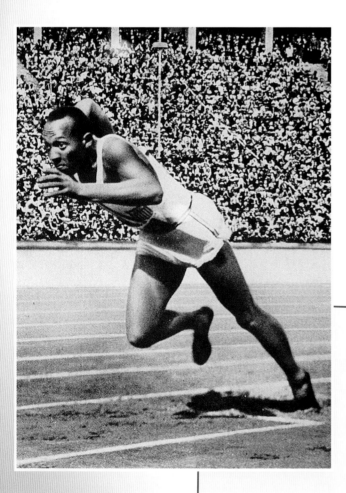

### ENTER JESSE OWENS
By the time of the 11th Games in 1936, James 'Jesse' Owens was already a living legend. The year before, at an American championship, he had broken three world records and equalled a fourth – all in the space of 45 minutes.

News of this fabulous feat stunned the world. But surely he would have a hard job living up to everyone's expectations at the Berlin Olympics?

◀ The magnificent Jesse Owens. In 1936 he was asked for the secret of his success by a London reporter. 'I let my feet spend as little time as possible on the ground,' Owens replied. 'From the air, fast down, and from the ground, fast up. My foot is only a fraction of the time on the track.'

He would also have to run and jump there in a very odd atmosphere. Germany's ruling **Nazi** Party was trying hard to convince everyone that athletes from the white German 'master race' were 'superior' to those from any other. They saw the Olympic Games as an opportunity to demonstrate their racist theory.

However, Jesse Owens won the 100 metres, the 200 metres, the long jump, and the sprint relay – and in the words of one rival, he made it all look as easy and inevitable as 'water running downhill'. At the time, few people would have guessed that Owens' four-gold-medal achievement would ever be equalled at a later Games.

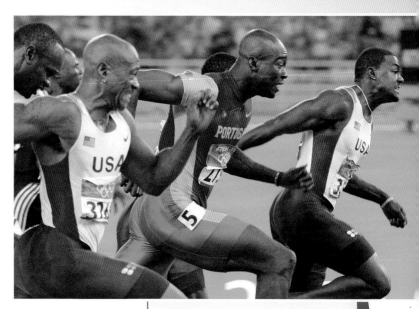

Justin Gatlin (right) of the United States, won the gold medal in the 100 metres during the 2004 Olympic Games in Athens.

## REPEAT PERFORMER

In 1984 at Los Angeles, Carl Lewis won gold in exactly the same four events as Jesse Owens. Owens had won the 100 metres in 10.3 seconds. Lewis won in 9.99 seconds and by a margin of eight feet – the widest in Olympic history. In the 1988 Olympics, Lewis won the 100 metres and long jump again – which no man had ever done before. Four years later in Barcelona, he won his seventh and eighth gold medals in the long jump and sprint relay.

### FAST AND FURIOUS

In a sprint race, the difference between a gold, silver, and bronze medal can be tiny. In Athens in 2004, it was just one hundredth of a second.

| | | |
|---|---|---|
| Justin Gatlin | USA | 9.85 seconds |
| Francis Obikwelu | Portugal | 9.86 seconds |
| Maurice Greene | USA | 9.87 seconds |

This was the first time that five men finished in under 10 seconds in one 100-metre race at an Olympic Games.

# FABULOUS FINNS

The Olympic all-time medals table is topped by the USA. You might have expected that. It is a big, rich country which has always taken the training of its athletes very seriously. Its **Cold War** rival the **USSR** – in second place – turned the making of Olympic champions into a kind of industry. Then come several European nations, like Germany and Italy, with a long history of sporting excellence. But just behind them is a rather surprising country: Finland.

## THE DRIVING FORCE OF SISU

Between 1912 and 1936 Finland's track athletes won 24 gold medals. This was an extraordinary achievement for a nation which numbers only five million people today. A second great age of Olympic success opened up for the Finns at Munich in 1972 – and then, as before, they did best at long and middle-distance running.

Why was this? No one can say for sure. But the Finns themselves talk of a national characteristic called *sisu* – a single-minded mixture of pride and guts and the sheer will to win. Perhaps it had something to do with that.

### FINLAND'S MEDALS

**As of the 2006 Turin Games, Finland has won 102 gold, 84 silver, and 115 bronze medals in the Summer Olympics. In the Winter Olympics they have won 42 gold, 57 silver, and 51 bronze medals**

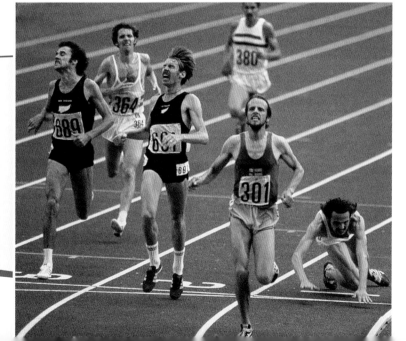

Lasse Virén (in front): one of a long line of great Finnish distance runners. ▶

Finnish athletes have excelled at the javelin, as well as long-distance running. In the men's event, Finns have won seven Olympic titles since World War One.

In the women's event, Ilse 'Tiina' Lillak won the 1983 World Championship with a last-round throw of 70 m 82 cm (232 feet 4 inches) – a new world record. Only an injury to her right foot stopped her from winning the Olympic title at Los Angeles in 1984 too. ▶

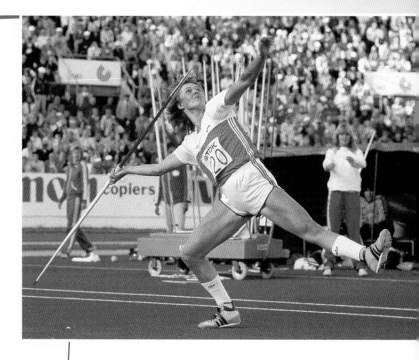

## FINNISH FLYERS

From 1920 to 1928, carpenter's son Paavo Nurmi was so far ahead of his rivals that his main challenge came from beating his own previous time. In fact he ran carrying a stopwatch, to improve his pace judgement even further! He won nine Olympic gold medals and broke 22 official world records in distances ranging from 1,500 metres to 20,000 metres. And when he left the scene, other distance-runners kept Finland high in the medals table until the outbreak of World War Two. Then, amazingly, from 1948 to 1972 the Finns did not win a single Olympic title. The man who changed all that was another **phenomenon** of the track: Lasse Virén.

This 23-year-old policeman won his first gold medal at Munich the hard way. In the middle of the 10,000 metres final Virén stumbled and fell. One of his main rivals, Mohamed Gammoudi, tripped on him, crashed to the ground, and left the race shortly after. Virén, though, got up and carried on – all the way to the gold medal, in a brand new world record time of 27 minutes 38.4 seconds. He then won the 5,000 metres too. And at Montreal four years later, he not only repeated his double-gold performance, but he came fifth in the marathon as well! If any Finnish athlete had *sisu* to spare, it was Lasse Virén.

# TINY GYMNASTIC GIANTS

The sport of gymnastics has figured in every modern Games since 1896. But, as in most Olympic sports, women's competitions took longer to arrive than men's. At Amsterdam in 1928 the first women's gymnastic team event took place. Then, in 1952, women's individual apparatus was introduced. So the stage was set for some of the most memorable Olympic champions of all – many of them coming from the countries of eastern Europe.

## EASTERN EUROPEAN GOLD

At the 1972 Games, the world met 'The Munchkin of Munich' – an **elfin** seventeen-year-old gymnast from the **USSR** called Olga Korbut. She was only 150 centimetres (59 inches) tall and weighed just 39 kilograms (86 pounds). Her mischievous smile entranced millions. She was also popular with the judges, who awarded her three gold medals even though some experts questioned her technique. Her team-mate, nineteen-year-old Lyudmila Tourischeva, won the all-round title. Four years later another young Soviet gymnast, Nelli Kim, received two perfect scores of 10 for her performances. Even so, she did not manage to win the all-round crown.

Olga Korbut – darling of the world's **media** at Munich in 1972. When she went for a walk during the Games, buses stopped so that passengers could get out and ask for autographs. On returning home to Grodno in the USSR, she got so much fan mail that a clerk was employed just to deal with letters for her. ▶

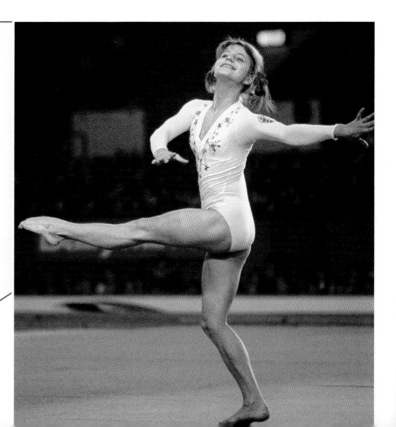

The champion that year in Montreal was Romania's awesome Nadia Comaneci. Only fourteen years of age, she had been trained as a gymnast since the age of six. She scored 10s from all seven judges on both the parallel bars and the balance beam. Unprepared for such a gymnastic genius, the electronic scoreboard could show nothing higher than 9.95. And for Comaneci's performance it registered only 1.00. But she knew she had achieved perfection. Four years later, as a 'veteran' of eighteen, she dazzled again at Moscow, and her final haul of Olympic medals was nine – five of them gold.

## US CHAMPIONS

The United States has also had its tiny gymnastic giants. Mary Lou Retton won the gold medal in the women's all-round competition at the 1984 Olympic Games in Los Angeles. Twenty years later Carly Patterson did the same in the Athens Olympic Games. She also won two silver medals, one in the team competition and one on the balance beam.

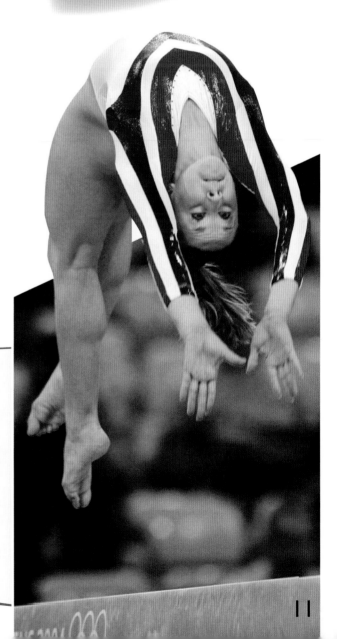

**Carly Patterson**

**Height**: 144.8 cm (4 feet 9 inches)
**Born**: 4 February 1988
**Hometown**: Baton Rouge, Louisiana, USA
**Resides**: Allen, Texas, USA
**Sport:** Gymnastics
**Favourite event**: Balance beam ▶

# LEAPS OF THE CENTURY

Someone once said that Olympic records are like piecrusts – they are meant to be broken. Since 1896, more than 50 percent of the finals of **track and field** events have been won with a record-breaking performance. The figure for swimming is over 70 percent. In some Olympic events, however, records tend to stand for a very long time. In the case of the men's long jump, it can seem like an eternity.

At Berlin in 1936 super-athlete Jesse Owens (see page 6) took the long jump gold medal, setting a new **Olympic record** of 8.06 metres. But he could not beat the world record he had set the year before. On that day in Michigan, just before Owens jumped for the first time, an announcer told the crowd: 'Jesse Owens will now attempt a new long-jump world's record.' And he did it, with a leap of 8.13 metres! His record stood until fellow-American Ralph Boston broke it ... in 1960.

Bob Beamon makes his massive leap at the Mexico City Games of 1968. He jumped beyond the range of the officials' state-of-the-art measuring device, so an old-fashioned steel tape had to be called for.

## DIZZY HEIGHTS FOR LONG-JUMPERS

Before the Mexico Games of 1968, everyone was talking about the city's high **altitude**. The thin air, they thought, would surely have a bad effect on the breathing of long-distance runners. But no one predicted the *good* effect it would have on specialists in the more explosive events – like the long jump.

The three medallists from the Tokyo Games four years earlier were competing again: Lynn Davies (UK), Ralph Boston (USA), and Igor Ter-Ovanesyan (**USSR**). Everyone wondered which of them would win the gold. But an outsider struggled through the qualifying round to compete against them in the final.

He was Bob Beamon, a 22 year-old from New York, USA, who stood 190 centimetres (6 feet 3 inches) tall. He could run like the wind, but often had trouble hitting the take-off board properly. The crowd gasped when he suddenly took off perfectly and sailed through the air at almost his own height, then landed so hard that he bounced back up and landed outside the pit!

## 'YOU HAVE DESTROYED THIS EVENT'

How far had Beamon gone? The electronic scoreboard showed a distance of 8.9 metres. It was stupendous. But until the metric measurement was converted into feet and inches, the jumper himself did not fully realise what he had done. No one in history had ever achieved a 28 feet (8.5 metres) jump, let alone 29 feet, two and a half inches (8.9 metres)! Thinking that no one would ever be able to beat that record, a dazed Lynn Davies said to the new champion, 'You have destroyed this event.' He was not quite right. In 1991, Mike Powell finally surpassed Beamon's world-record mark in a non-Olympic competition. But the freak jump of 1968 still stands as an Olympic record.

### HIGH JUMP FLOPS

Unlike the long jump, the high jump did not figure in the ancient Greek Games, but in modern times it is often a breathtakingly exciting event. American Dick Fosbury changed its nature forever in Mexico City when he won gold with his new head-first and backwards style of clearing the bar. The 'Fosbury Flop' later became the standard style for high-jumpers, but in 1968 it looked very risky. Fosbury's coach warned, 'If kids imitate Fosbury he will wipe out an entire generation of jumpers because they will all have broken necks.'

# AMAZING AFRICANS

Until 1960 no black African athlete had won a **track-and-field** gold medal. That all changed at the Rome Olympics, thanks to an Ethiopian bodyguard called Abebe Bikila.

## MARATHON MARVEL

The 1960 marathon was staged at night, when the temperature was cooler. The race started and ended outside the stadium. It was only the third time Abebe Bikila had run a marathon in his life. He won – barefoot – in a time of 2 hours 15 minutes 16.2 seconds. Four years later, Bikila proved that his victory was no accident. Only 40 days before the Tokyo marathon, he had his appendix removed. He still finished in a record time of 2 hours 12 minutes 11.2 seconds. He even ran a lap of honour before the next runner, Britain's Basil Heatley, appeared in the stadium.

## AFRICANS AT ALTITUDE

At Mexico City in 1968 another Ethiopian, 36-year-old Mamo Wolde, won the marathon. More than an hour after he broke the tape, John Akhwari of Tanzania entered the stadium. He had hurt himself badly in a fall but struggled on through the pain. 'My country did not send me 7,000 miles to start the race,' he said afterwards. 'They sent me 7,000 miles to finish it.'

◀ At Barcelona in 1992 the women's 10,000 m was a race to remember. After the 6,000 m mark, South African Elana Meyer took the lead. Derartu Tulu of Ethiopia went with her. Soon these two were so far ahead that no one else could catch them. Lap after lap Tulu ran just behind Meyer. Then with 420 m to go, she eased in front, stormed away and won by a full 30 m.

For the first time ever, a black African woman had won an Olympic medal. And Meyer's silver was South Africa's first medal since her country had been banned after the 1960 Games. They set off hand in hand for a shared victory lap.

In Mexico City, African runners took gold in all races from 1,500 metres to the marathon. In the 5,000 metres, uncoached Kenyan 'Kip' Keino lost by a hair's breadth to Tunisia's Mohamed Gammoudi. In the 1,500 metres, he won the gold, even though he had to run to the stadium before the race because he had been caught in a traffic jam.

Keino was up against world-record-holder Jim Ryun of the USA. He had also been suffering from violent stomach pains. You would not have known it as, at the finish, Keino took the gold by beating Ryun by 20 metres, the largest-ever margin of victory in this event. At Munich four years later Keino was beaten into second place in the 1,500 metres by Pekka Vasala of Finland. But he decided to enter the 3,000-metre steeplechase too, as a challenge. In this event – featuring 28 hurdles and seven water jumps – Keino had little experience, and he admitted that he jumped 'like an animal'. But he was still good enough to win the gold medal, and set an Olympic record time of 8 minutes 23.6 seconds in beating everyone else in sight.

## CAN YOU BELIEVE IT?

African runners won all three medals in the 10,000 metres at Athens in 2004. There were just four seconds between the first two Ethiopian runners. The winner, Kenenisa Bekele, ran even faster the following year in Belgium, finishing in just 26 minutes 17.53 seconds!

| | | |
|---|---|---|
| Kenenisa Bekele | Ethiopia | 27:05.10 |
| Sileshi Sihine | Ethiopia | 27:09.39 |
| Zersenay Tadesse | Eritrea | 27:22.57 |

Kenenisa Bekele (left) broke the Olympic record for 10,000 m in the 2004 Olympics.

# FOOTBALL STARS

The football World Cup began in 1930. Until then, the winners of the Olympic football tournament could rightly be called the champions of the world. Only five countries entered the first full tournament, at the 1908 Games, and it was won by England. The 1920 final between host nation Belgium and Czechoslovakia was a bad-tempered affair. The Czech team – trailing 2–0 and feeling that the referee was favouring the home side – simply walked off the field after half an hour!

## TRUE WORLD CHAMPIONS

At the 1924 Games in Paris, many Europeans were able to watch a dazzling South American team for the first time. That team was Uruguay, and they took the tournament by storm, beating Switzerland 3–0 in the final to take the gold.

◄ The last Olympic champions who could also be called true world champions were Hungary in 1952. Featuring stars like Hidegkuti, Kocsis, and Puskas (on the left), they scored 20 goals and conceded only two in winning the 1952 tournament.

Virtually the same team then played in the 1954 World Cup Final against West Germany. Earlier in the competition they had already thrashed the Germans 8–3, yet to everyone's amazement they managed to lose the final 2–3.

| OLYMPIC FOOTBALL CHAMPIONS |
| --- |
| Since the first full Olympic soccer tournament in 1908, these have been the winners: |
| **MEN** |
| 1908 England |
| 1912 Sweden |
| 1920 Belgium |
| 1924 Uruguay |
| 1928 Uruguay |
| 1936 Italy |
| 1948 Sweden |
| 1952 Hungary |
| 1956 USSR |
| 1960 Yugoslavia |
| 1964 Hungary |
| 1968 Hungary |
| 1972 Poland |
| 1976 East Germany |
| 1980 Czechoslovakia |
| 1984 France |
| 1988 USSR |
| 1992 Spain |
| 1996 Nigeria (men); USA (women) |
| 2000 Cameroon (men); Norway (women) |
| 2004 Argentina (men); USA (women) |

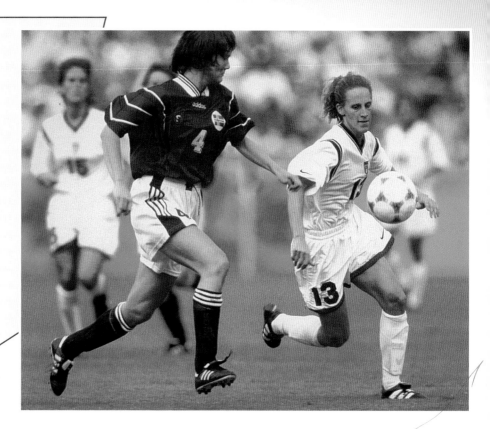

The US women's soccer team (in all white), who won the first Olympic gold medal in their sport in 1996. They are shown here beating Norway in the semi-finals. ▶

Four years later, in Amsterdam, the Uruguayans were back, along with the Argentinians, also from South America. The Argentinians thrashed the USA 11–2, beat Belgium 6–3, then crushed Egypt 6–0 on route to the final. There they met … Uruguay! After the first match ended in a draw, Uruguay won the replay 2–1 to retain their Olympic title. Few could doubt that they were the best team in the world. When the first World Cup was held – in Uruguay – in 1930, they won that too.

In 1936 in Berlin, recent World-Cup-winners Italy also won the gold. But by that time so many of the world's footballers were **professional** that many nations had to send under-strength squads to the **amateur** Olympics. And during the **Cold War** period, the **Communist** countries of eastern Europe dominated the tournament, combining great skill with strong government support.

## PROFESSIONALS ALLOWED IN

After 1984, professional players who had not competed in World Cup games were allowed to take part in the Olympics. Soccer at the Games continued to draw huge crowds. In 1984 and 1988 more spectators watched soccer than any other event, including athletics. Then in 1992, at Barcelona, the rules changed again: the Olympic soccer tournament became the official competition for all the world's under-23-year-old teams.

# REPEAT PERFORMANCES

To win a gold medal in any Olympic event is a supreme achievement. To go back four years later and win again is quite staggering. But to be the Olympic champion a third time, even a *fourth* time, that seems almost unbelievable. It takes a very special person indeed to be the world's best for a period of sixteen years. Yet it has happened....

## ONE-MAN GOLD RUSHES

Ray Ewry of the USA won a record ten gold medals in the now-discontinued 'standing jumps' between 1900 and 1908 – in spite of the fact that Ewry had suffered from polio as a boy. Russian triple-jumper Viktor Saneyev won his event in 1968, 1972, and 1976. Then in 1980, at the age of 34, he failed by only 11 centimetres to add a fourth gold medal to his career total.

But by then, one man had already achieved that stupendous feat. He was Paul Elvstrom of Denmark, who won his four consecutive gold medals in the Finn class of the yachting competitions between 1948 and 1960. At the Helsinki Games of 1952, he was already so many points ahead that he did not have to race on the last day. But he entered anyway – and won that race too!

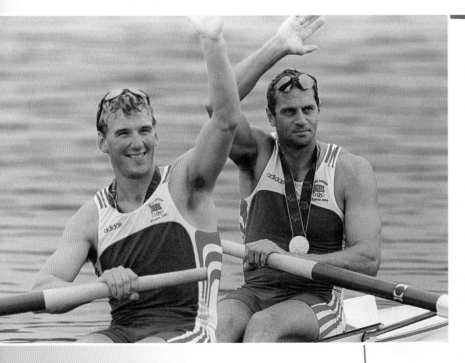

◀ British oarsman Steven Redgrave (right) is the only rower to win gold medals in five consecutive Olympics. He began his amazing record at the 1984 Los Angeles Games as a member of the British coxed fours crew. Sixteen years later, at the age of 38, he won a fifth gold medal at the 2000 Olympics, this time as a member of the British coxless fours team.

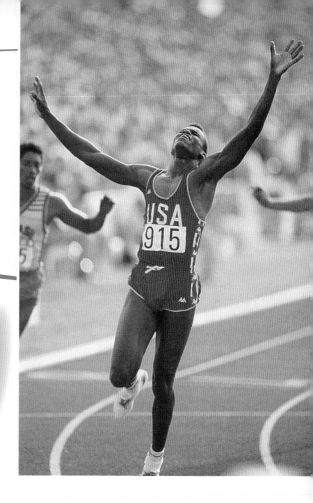

Carl Lewis of the United States was not just a world-record-beating sprinter, but a fabulous long-jumper, too. In Atlanta, Georgia, in 1996, he won the Olympic long jump for the fourth time. ▶

## NOT JUST MEN

Over a 24-year period (1980–2004), German canoe champion Birgit Fischer won eight gold medals in a record six different Olympic Games! At 18 she was the youngest ever Olympic canoeing champion, and aged 42 she became the oldest ever canoeing champion. That's some record!

## THE ULTIMATE COMPETITOR

Discus-thrower Al Oerter won the same Olympic **track-and-field** event four times, in 1956, 1960, 1964, and 1968. When he won his first gold with a new Olympic record, the truth did not sink in until he was up on the victory **rostrum**. Then his knees buckled and he almost fell off.

He had plenty of time to get used to standing at that dizzy height. But Oerter was more than just a great thrower, he was a great competitor. Three times he had to beat the current world-record holder to win gold. Three times he produced a lifetime-best throw to set the winning mark. And at Tokyo in 1964, he injured his lower ribs so badly while practising that doctors told him to forget about competing. But it took more than that to stop him. With his fifth throw, as he doubled up in pain, he set a new Olympic record to win the event. 'These are the Olympics,' the hero explained afterwards. 'You die for them.'

# PICK OF THE POOL

## GREG LOUGANIS – SPRINGBOARD AND PLATFORM KING

Only two divers have won the springboard and platform events at two different Olympic Games. The first was Patricia McCormick of the United States in 1952 and 1956 – and she won the latter pair of golds only eight months after giving birth to a son. The second was fellow American Greg Louganis in 1984 and 1988. Louganis had a tough early life. He recovered from being a teenage **alcoholic**, but he was so good at diving that he qualified for the 1976 Games when aged only sixteen. On the springboard in 1984 his winning margin of 92 points was the biggest in Olympic history.

Four years later in Seoul, he hit his head on the springboard during the preliminary round. But still he went on to win the final. Then he had to face fourteen-year-old **prodigy** Xiong Ni from China in the platform final. It was neck and neck until Louganis' last dive, known as the "Dive of Death" because two men had died trying to make it. Louganis survived – and won.

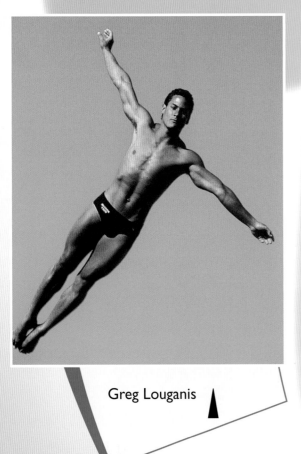

Greg Louganis

## JOHNNY WEISSMULLER – KING OF THE WATER, LORD OF THE APES

As a child, Romanian-born American Johnny Weissmuller was believed to have heart problems. But he grew up to become the first person to swim the 100 metres in less than a minute (in 1922). At the Paris Games of 1924, he won three gold medals, and he went on to keep his 100 metre title at Amsterdam in 1928. His style was extremely relaxed: 'I didn't tense up,' he explained. After retiring from the pool, he took up acting and became a famous Hollywood Tarzan, starring in many films. Three other Olympic medallists also played that movie role!

## DAWN FRASER – AUSTRALIA'S RECORD-BREAKER

Dawn Fraser was 19 years old in 1956 when she won a gold medal in her native Australia, for swimming 100 metres in a record 1 minute 2 seconds. She won gold again in the next Olympics in Rome and the next in Tokyo in 1964. No other Olympic swimmer had ever won the same.

Dawn Fraser

## 2004 POOL PRESSURE

Rivalry in the pool between Australia and the USA was never so intense than at the 2004 Olympics. It produced some outstanding and exciting swimming from Ian Thorpe of Australia and Michael Phelps of the USA.

Thorpe had won three gold medals in 2000 and took two more in 2004, the most won by any Australian. Phelps broke even more records in 2004 by becoming the first American to win eight medals (six gold and two bronze) in the same Olympics. Like Mark Spitz 32 years before, he won four individual events in one Games. Phelps became the first swimmer in history to qualify for the Olympic Games in six individual events!

## MARK SPITZ – MOST-GOLDEN OLYMPIAN

American swimmer Mark Spitz began his glittering Olympic career at Mexico City in 1968 – and went home with four medals: two golds for relays and a silver and a bronze for individual events. That was pretty good. But at Munich four years later he rewrote the record books. He won *seven* gold medals there in all, the most ever won at a single Games. More astonishing still, he won every gold medal in a new world-record time. His father would have been pleased. 'Swimming isn't everything,' he had told Mark as a boy, 'winning is.'

# SUPREME STRONGMEN

## ALEXANDER MEDVED – SOVIET WRESTLING SENSATION

Russian freestyle wrestler Alexander Medved has been called the greatest wrestler of the 20<sup>th</sup> century – and even of the past 2,000 years! The mighty wrestlers of ancient times would probably have found this nimble bear of a man hard to beat. As a light-heavyweight and then as a super-heavyweight, he won three Olympic titles between 1964 and 1972. He also won seven world championships in three weight divisions between 1962 and 1972. Rarely weighing more than his opponent, he won by speed, power, and intelligence.

## NAIM SULEYMANOGLU – TURKEY'S 'POCKET HERCULES'

Featherweight weightlifter Naim Suleymanoglu was born in Bulgaria but his family was Turkish. Although not quite 150 centimetres (4.9 feet) tall, he was immensely strong. At the age of fourteen he came within 2.5 kilogrammes (5.5 pounds) of breaking the *adult* world record for combined lifts, and by the age of sixteen he was lifting three times his own body weight. In 1984 he was too young to compete for Bulgaria at the Los Angeles Olympics. But four years later he did appear – in the *Turkish* team. (In 1986 he had **defected**; and for a fee of more than £500,000 from the Turkish government, the government of Bulgaria let him change his nationality.)

In Seoul he won Turkey's first gold medal for 20 years. Girls had used to laugh at him for being so short. Now he was a national sex symbol! He wanted to retire while still at the top but was persuaded to keep competing. This turned out to be a good idea. He won in Barcelona and again in Atlanta, thus becoming weightlifting's first triple Olympic champion in three successive Games.

## CASSIUS CLAY – THE BEST AND THE PRETTIEST (OR SO HE SAID!)

No boxer ever talked a better fight – or fought one – than Cassius Marcellus Clay – winner of the light-heavyweight gold at Rome in 1960. Eighteen at the time, he was so proud of his medal that he wore it all the time, even sleeping with it, so that the gold plating began to come off. He later turned **professional** and won the world heavyweight championship in 1964, before converting to Islam and changing his name to Muhammad Ali. A uniquely talented sportsman, he was one of the world's most famous people during the 1960s and 1970s.

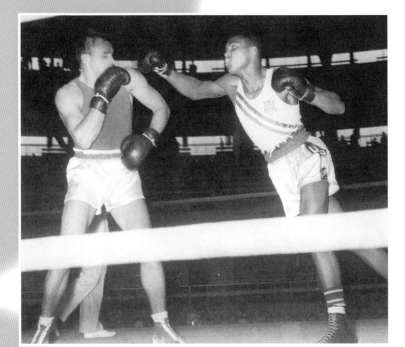

## YASUHIRO YAMASHITA – JAPAN'S BIG FRIDGE!

At almost 180 cm (5 ft 9 in) in height and weighing 125 kg (276 lbs), judo open champion Yasuhiro Yamashita from Japan was described by one opponent as 'a refrigerator with a head on top'. After losing in the final of the Japanese Student Championships in 1977, he did not lose one of his next 194 matches at national and international level! He won his Olympic title in 1984 with such a bad leg injury that his opponent had to help him up to the top step to receive his gold medal.

## NOT JUST FOR MEN

Supremely strong women are also part of today's Olympics. In Athens in 2004, China's Tang Gonghong was crowned the strongest woman in the world. She won the gold medal for lifting a massive 305 kg (672 lbs) – that's more than a large motorbike, or a fully grown male tiger!

# YESTERDAY'S SUPERSTARS

All Olympics have their stars, but some individuals have been exceptional. One was a mother of two children who won four gold medals in the 1948 Olympics in London. These were the first Games after a long break during World War Two. It was a time when sport needed a boost, even though many people disregarded women's athletics altogether. But one woman, Fanny Blankers-Koen from the Netherlands, was to prove the critics wrong. She became known as 'The Flying Housewife'.

The crowd roared as Fanny won one race after another: 100 metres, 200 metres, and the 80-metre hurdles. Then came the 4 x 100-metre relay, where Fanny had to run the last leg of the race. When she took the baton, the Dutch team was fourth and their chances were poor. There seemed to be no way she could pass three runners in such a short distance. But Fanny had other ideas. She sped past them and on to break the tape, becoming the first woman to win four track and field golds – all at the same Games.

When Fanny (far right) got home she was treated as a huge star. Her friends gave her a bicycle so she wouldn't have to run so much! Fanny died in 2004 when she was 85 years old. ▼

Between 1948 and 1954, Emil Zatopek (on the right) won 38 10,000-metre races in a row and often won by huge margins. Years later, he was asked why he looked so pained when he ran. 'I was not talented enough to run and smile at the same time,' he replied. ▶

## YOU CAN'T CATCH ZATOPEK

Emil Zatopek may not have run with style but he was one of the all-time Olympic greats. From Czechoslovakia, he was the first athlete to run the 10,000 metres in less than 29 minutes. He is widely considered to be one of the greatest runners of the 20th century and was also known for his merciless training methods.

It was in the Helsinki Olympics of 1952 that Zatopek became a real star. As if winning gold in both the 5,000 metres and the 10,000 metres wasn't enough, he was set to run the marathon. When his wife won a gold medal in the javelin, Zatopek told reporters, "The score of the contest in the Zatopek family is 2–1. This result is too close. To restore some prestige I will try to improve on the margin in the marathon." He did it, too!

After 15 kilometres (9 miles), he was in the lead alongside Britain's Jim Peters. Six weeks before, Peters had run the fastest marathon in history. Zatopek had never run a marathon in his life. He turned to Peters and asked, "The pace, is it fast enough?" Peters had started too quickly, and now he felt exhausted. But he did not want Zatopek to know that, so he replied, "No, it's too slow." Zatopek thought about this, then raced ahead to a stunning victory.

Zatopek's triple-gold haul in Helsinki was a magnificent achievement. He became a hero back in Prague until his death in 2000 at the age of 78.

# WINTER WONDERS

## SONJA HENIE – CHILD SKATING STAR

Norway's Sonja Henie was the greatest female figure skater in the world for more than a decade – and she remains the most successful, individual, woman skater in Olympic history. At the first Winter Olympics in 1924 she took part as an eleven-year-old. She won no medals at Chamonix, but thanks in part to seven hours of training each day, she never lost a competition after the age of thirteen. The winner of ten figure-skating world championships in a row, she was also the Olympic gold medallist in 1928, 1932, and 1936. Her **repertoire** for the time was breathtaking, including a whirl with up to 80 spins.

## JEAN-CLAUDE KILLY – 'KILLYMPIC HERO'

The star of the 1968 Winter Olympics at Grenoble was Alpine-skier Jean-Claude Killy. In the downhill event, in the slalom, and also in the giant slalom, the 24-year-old Frenchman turned in gold-medal-winning performances. Like Torvill and Dean in Britain, he became an immensely popular hero in his own country; and after helping to organise the 1992 Winter Games he joined the International Olympic Committee in 1995.

## COOL RUNNINGS

Most Winter Olympic teams come from countries where there is plenty of ice and snow. But at Calgary in 1988, there was a four-man bobsleigh team from ... Jamaica! The Jamaicans did not win a medal, but it was a great achievement to qualify for the Games in the first place. The Walt Disney Corporation certainly thought so. They made a successful film about the team, Cool Runnings.

## TORVILL AND DEAN – INCOMPARABLE ICE DANCERS

By the time of the 1984 Games in Sarajevo, Britain's Jayne Torvill and Christopher Dean had already been the world ice-dance champions for three years. Their performances at the Olympics then took their sport to a new level of achievement. For their interpretation of Ravel's *Bolero*, all nine judges awarded them the maximum 6 points for artistic presentation. In the whole competition, they gained twelve 6s out of a possible eighteen.

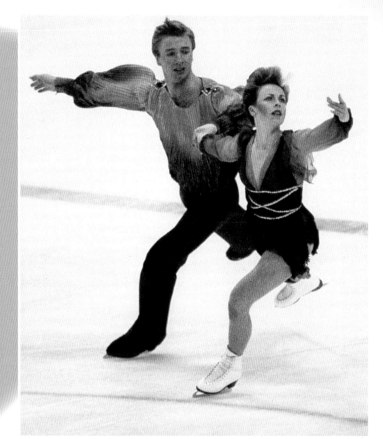

## ERIC HEIDEN – CLEAN SWEEP SPEED SKATER

At the opening of the 1980 Winter Olympics in Lake Placid, USA, the Olympic oath was taken by Eric Heiden, the 21-year-old American speed skater. He stayed in the headlines by making a clean sweep of the five speed-skating gold medals, all in Olympic record times – and in the 10,000 m he set a new world record. Just for good measure, his sister Beth also won a bronze in the 3,000 m event for women.

## HELPING HAND

In the 2006 Winter Olympics in Turin, Canadian Sara Renner broke one of her poles in the cross-country skiing team sprint, but a Norwegian coach came to her rescue! Bjørnar Håkensmoen gave her one of his poles, even though it was 12 centimetres (5 inches) too long. This allowed Renner to help her team win silver medals, and pushed Norway into fourth place. Bjørnar Håkensmoen's display of fair play showed great Olympic spirit.

# BEYOND BELIEF

At one time it would have been unbelievable that women or athletes with physical disabilities would ever take part in the Olympics! But in the 21st century there have been many great Olympic moments when athletes of every kind have pushed themselves to the limit, to the thrill of the billions of TV viewers around the world.

One of the great moments for British viewers of the 2004 Athens Olympics was when Kelly Holmes won gold medals in both the 800 metres and the 1,500 metres. British Olympic chief Simon Clegg paid tribute to her achievement when he said, 'It is unbelievable. I think she has run two perfect races and that's why I asked her to carry the flag at the closing ceremony.'

## 2004'S GOLDEN WOMEN

In the women's pole vault, Yelena Isinbayeva broke her own world record and won gold. The Russian cleared 4.91 metres (16.1 feet), one centimetre (0.4 inches) over her previous world record! Americans Kerri Walsh and Misty May won the women's beach volleyball, with the bronze going to another American team. This was the first US success in this women's sport, which was first held in the 1996 Olympics.

Kelly Holmes celebrates winning the 1500 metres final at the 2004 Olympics in Athens. ▼

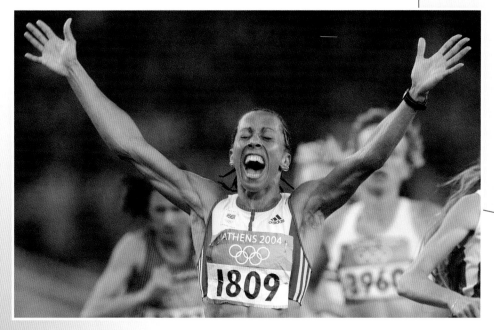

# PARALYMPIC STARS

Who would have believed, when the first Paralympic Games were held in Rome in 1960 for athletes with disabilities, that the 21st century would see the Games achieving the size, standard and prestige they now have?

The Athens 2004 Paralympic Games brought together the world's best athletes with a disability. Out of the 136 competing nations, 73 won at least one medal. Some amazing performances in 19 sports produced 304 world records and 448 Paralympic records. In the final medal tally for the 2004 Paralympics, China was top. The 2008 Olympic host won 141 medals, 63 of which were gold. Great Britain finished second overall, with 35 gold medals, followed by Canada with 28 gold.

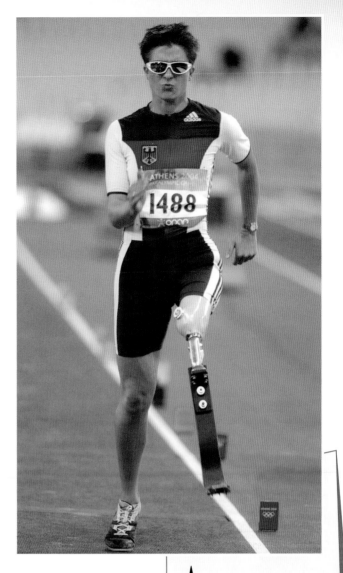

▲ Germany's Christine Wolf competes in the women's long jump final at the Athens 2004 Paralympic Games.

One of the most outstanding athletes at the 2004 Paralympic Games was Japanese swimmer Mayumi Narita, who won seven gold medals and one bronze. Narita has been in a wheelchair since the age of 13. In 1994, friends encouraged her to take part in a swimming competition for people with a disability, even though she couldn't swim! After just one month of training, she won the competition. Narita was later involved in a traffic accident that made her **quadriplegic**. But she didn't give in; she persisted with her training and, after several months, returned to competitive swimming, and to great success!

# GLOSSARY

**alcoholic**  person who is addicted to drinking alcohol

**altitude**  height above sea level

**amateur**  someone who competes for fun, rather than as a job, and who is unpaid

**Cold War**  period, after World War Two, of unfriendly relations between the United States and USSR, which never quite became head-to-head conflict

**Communism**  idea that a single, ruling political party can provide for all its people better than if they are left to make their own decisions and keep their own homes, land, and businesses. The USSR became the first Communist state in 1917. After World War Two, the USSR introduced Communism into much of eastern Europe.

**defected**  left one country to live in another, without official permission

**elfin**  small and attractive (like an elf)

**Islam**  Muslim religion

**media**  plural of medium (of communication), for example newspapers, magazines, TV, and radio

**Nazi**  short form of the National Socialist German Workers' Party, a political party led by Adolf Hitler during World War Two

**phenomenon**  remarkable person, thing or event

**prodigy**  someone, especially a child, who is very talented

**professional**  paid competitor

**quadriplegic**  person who has lost the use of their arms and legs

**rationed**  when food and other materials are scarce, such as during and just after World War Two, they are distributed by an official system, so no one gets more than their share

**repertoire**  range of skills that a person has

**rostrum**  victory platform

**track and field**  sporting events which involve running, jumping, throwing and walking – such as the 100 metres or the javelin

**USSR**  Communist country, which included Russia and many smaller nations, that broke up in 1991

# FIND OUT MORE

## USING THE INTERNET

Explore the Internet to find out more about the history of great Olympic moments or to see pictures of the most recent Games. You can use a search engine such as www.yahooligans.com, or ask a question at www.ask.com. To find out more about great Olympic moments, you could search by typing in key words such as Olympic records, great Olympians, or Paralympics.

These are some useful websites to look at to find more information:

http://www.databaseolympics.com/index.htm
This database lists medal winners from all Olympic Games.

http://www.hickoksports.com/history/olympix.shtml
This website lists Olympic records through time.

http://www.infoplease.com/spot/olympicstimeline.html
This website provides a timeline of the Olympics.

http://www.olympic.org
This is the official website of the Olympic Movement, with all the latest news and a countdown to the next Games.

## BOOKS

*Amazing Pace: The Story of Olympic Champion Michael Phelps from Sydney to Athens to Beijing,* Paul McMullen (Rodale Books, USA, 2006)

*My Olympic Ten Days,* Kelly Holmes with Richard Lewis (Virgin Books, 2004)

*The Olympics: Facts, Figures and Fun,* Liam McCann (Artists' and Photographers' Press, 2006)

# INDEX